A Guide to Grieving Well

Invitation *to* Tears

Jonalyn Fincher
Aubrie Hills

soulationPRESS

Deep calls to deep at the sound of Your waterfalls;
All Your breakers and Your waves have rolled over me.

Psalm 42:7

Table *of* Contents

Foreword

That morning my family could see his last boot tracks. From the sidewalk to the front door of the house, John's tracks remained planted—his last trip home carved into the fallen snow.

Those tracks marked the last trace of John's life. The night before, at the bathroom sink, my great grandfather fell dead of a heart attack. The next morning, when more family arrived to help, they paused at the boot tracks in the snow.

Four generations later, my family still tells the story of those tracks.

Tracks of our ancestors string behind us in a long line. Every person of each generation influenced, loved, worked, suffered, worshipped, and died. We keep the tracks going. We make our own tracks, often picking up where other's stopped.

Their blood also runs in our veins, their love in our souls. When those who loved us are gone, something shifts deep inside of us.

We have a name for that inner shift; we call it grief.

Grief, I've learned, is a downer at a dinner party and rarely part of small talk at church services. We don't know what to do with people who are suffering. Even if we want to help, we may feel like a bull in a china shop. Afraid of making a mess, we leave the duty to others to knock on the door beyond the frozen boot tracks.

Passing by on the other side is not the lesson we learn from Jesus. But grieving well isn't something that just naturally happens. We don't know how to engage others' or our own grief unless we have the tools, guidance, and permission. Yet, from the story of the Good Samaritan, we know that grief, when done well, brings healing and life.[1]

Facing grief and loss in our own lives is like facing a pop-quiz. We'd rather be absent from class that day. Looking at it another way, grief is the echo that something good is gone. The pain now is part of the happiness then.[2] This paradox of loss is that our sadness is tied to our happiness. The pain of the pop-quiz is part of the joy of learning something: we have been happy, even if we are no longer.

Each of us has a list of grief—dysfunctional homes, abuse, failures, lost loves, lost opportunities, and lost lives. *Invitation to Tears* offers a chance not to compare the length of our lists, but to face the grief as it comes to us. How do we acknowledge what is good? How do we sit in this dark place without unraveling? How do we pause, move forward, and let our souls grow in the process?

Jonalyn Fincher and Aubrie Hills will help guide you to face your grief with dignity and power. Jonalyn

---

[1] All Scripture from the New International Version (2011) unless otherwise noted, Luke 10:33-35.

[2] An alteration of the line from Joy Lewis in *Shadowlands*, the film of the love and suffering of C. S. Lewis.

brings her philosophy and humanities training, along with a decade of ministering to hurting people. Aubrie brings her training and experience as a thanatologist, an expert on dying. Both are faithful companions for this journey. They are qualified and experienced in the school of grief. They will put a compass in your hand and teach you how to read its arrow. Heed these words and you will be navigating your way through these waters.

Let me offer a word of expectation: the journey through grief is a world absent of time. We each heal and process at different rates. Rushing to check grief off the list is a sure way to leave the work incomplete. Walking through the valley of the shadow with God, no matter how long the valley, is the only sure way forward.[3] Go with your hand in His. He is the captain of your vessel.

One day the snow of our grief will thaw and the boot tracks will fade. But you will carry the memories of what this loss has done to change your course. Your soul will be shaped to carry forward the legacy entrusted to you.

Dale Fincher
Spring 2014
Steamboat Springs, Colorado

[3] Psalm 23:4

Hoisting the Sails:
An Introduction

For many of us, grief is an unknown country. Some of us visit for weeks, others for years. Some of us attempt to steer back to what we've known. Some of us believe grief is wasteful, keeping us from practical tasks, like the work of being useful to God or checking off our bucket list. Grief is just too costly. So instead of charting toward a shadowed country, we take the swifter way around.

Instead of avoiding or fearing grief, we want to consider grief as a legitimate, God-honoring route through the seas of loss. Of all the sons of Adam, we've chosen one man as our captain to set our course. He was known for being "a man of suffering, and familiar with pain."[4] Jesus of Nazareth never shamed the downcast into cheering up; he neither rushed through nor avoided tears. On his walk to Golgotha, he directed the weeping women to cry for themselves and their children.[5] Even when Jesus could see the bluebird finish, the "man of sorrows" never took the sunny way around.[6] When Jesus prayed in Gethsemane, facing the impending loss of his life, we see his vulnerability as a suffering man. Grief brought Jesus to pray, "If it is possible, may this cup be taken from me."[7]

---

[4] Isaiah 53:3
[5] Luke 23:28
[6] Isaiah 53:3, NASB
[7] Matthew 26:39

We learn more about God and we learn more about ourselves when we enter grief.

But we also learn more about others who suffer. Paul explains in 2 Corinthians that the God who permits suffering in abundance will also comfort us in abundance.

> *We learn more about God and we learn more about ourselves when we enter grief.*

> Praise be to the God and Father of our Lord Jesus Christ, the Father of compassion and the God of all comfort, who comforts us in all our troubles, so that we can comfort those in any trouble with the comfort we ourselves receive from God. For just as we share abundantly in the sufferings of Christ, so also our comfort abounds through Christ.[8]

We are certain everyone's grief will be a unique story of the way God comforts. God's comfort multiplies. As we learn more about God's comfort through our loss, we are likewise prepared to deliver comfort to others.

We begin our journey with one clarification: we will talk about loss predominantly in terms of a death. We rely on the language of death because it describes a literal end of life and a metaphor for the end of a reality we knew. The death of a friendship, a job, a romance, a dream is just as important to grieve as the death of a person.

Climb aboard this ship called *grief* as we watch the land we knew grow small. We will not guarantee an end to your pain, but we will give you comfort that you are not alone. As we guide you into what grief can become, even as we are fallible guides, we want to show you territory we have both explored. We know a few refueling stations and when to lower the sails. We know that grief can change our agitated pace and make us more human. But, while all grief shares some similarities, our loss is not comparable to yours. We will not come skipping into your pain and deliver glib promises that if you just trim your sails like so, you'll be able to avoid that painful moment. Nor will we offer philosophical explanations and verses proving God is working this for good. The good that comes from any loss cannot erase or excuse it. Instead, we will offer our hand and hoist the sails into this unchartered territory with you.

With any good journey, you will want to stop from time to time. We've provided "Compass Checkpoints" as exercises for you to notice where you are, to put words to your location. You can skip the checkpoints if you like, but you will be more aware of the direction you're taking if you stop and check your compass. While we will explain grief and its processes, we will always remind you to calibrate with the God of comfort for his path for you.

Chapter 1
And So It Begins

*The world is indeed full of peril and in it there are
many dark places. But still there is much that is fair.
And though in all lands, love is now mingled with grief,
it still grows, perhaps, the greater.*
— J.R.R. Tolkien

The voyage into grief often begins with quiet seas,
a numbing stillness, ominous compared to the
agitation we know will ensue. Death comes almost as a
whisper, something we did not summon and cannot send
away.

In the rumbling of the first war for Middle Earth,
Gandalf quietly says, "And so it begins." Every grief is the
beginning of something different.

A mother learns that her pregnancy has ended,
before she even got comfortable with the idea of this new
life. She is a mother without a child.

A woman learns that she is pregnant and weeps. She
will not live child-free as she had hoped.

A college student pulls the ring off her finger,
replacing it in the quivering palm of her one-time fiancé.
They will never be man and wife.

A newlywed sits in the bathroom of her honeymoon

suite, no longer a virgin and no longer convinced sex is fun.

A man sits next to his childhood dog in the veterinarian office. Her suffering must be ended, but his is just beginning as memories flood his mind.

A son waits for God to take his mother's body, wracked with cancer, fighting for breath. With no living parents, he will now be an orphan.

A mother bumps into an old friend at the grocery store. For the first time since her daughter died, she must find a way to answer the question, "So how many children do you have?"

A friend opens her email to discover that her college roommate has been in a fatal car accident. She cannot remember the last time they connected. Now she won't get the chance.

Discover

Aubrie's colleague once shared the way she discovered grief. After shopping, she found a notice stuck to her windshield. She read the hand-written scrawl, "Your son was found dead this morning as a result of a car accident. Please call the police station for more information." The very medium of tape and paper on a car window refuses to dignify the depth of her loss.

Grief begins when we discover, even in a rushed note, that our normal is over. Grieving well means we honor the very first newsflash that our world is changed. From Jesus' life we know the way he honored grief, and it required more than a quick note.

At first, when Jesus' friend, Lazarus, is sick, he does something quite puzzling. He does what no one expects a caring friend to do: he stays away for two more days.[9] Later in the story, we see that God has bigger plans than we realize. Lazarus' famous return from the grave will be made all the *more* miraculous as each day passes.

But something else is presently going on for those back at home. As sisters Mary and Martha wash and wrap his body, painful and immediate decisions must be made for his burial, neighbors and family must be told that he is gone. And all the while, there is a mounting confusion and anger inside these sisters who don't always see eye to eye.[10] Jesus failed to come and heal their brother. They trusted Jesus. They knew his love personally. Mary anointed Jesus' feet and dried them with her hair.[11] These three were close.

> *There is a mounting confusion and anger inside these sisters who don't always see eye to eye.*

When Jesus finally arrives on the edge of the city, he's late, a sideshow interruption in the middle of the memorial service.

These devastated sisters go to Jesus and let their disappointment show. He could have prevented Lazarus' death. Jesus knows these sisters are understandably distracted. His eyes move across the sullen faces of black-

[9] John 11
[10] Luke 10:38-42
[11] 1 John 11:2

14

garmented mourners that have followed Mary to the tomb.

His response gives us the shortest verse in Scripture, "Jesus wept."[12]

How many times we have read these words and missed the significance. We've missed that Jesus' tears are a response to the living. They were not only for Lazarus. Jesus saw Lazarus' family and friends in communal mourning and their display of grieving moved him to weep. He discovers their changed reality and cries. He wasn't offering sympathy; he was feeling empathy as a human. He felt their loss and powerlessness.

He dignified the ceremony of grief by adding his own.

He honored their tears and disheveled appearance; he humbled himself by crying. The way we cry—covering our faces, our mouths, our eyes— proves how much we want to cover our own pain. Authentic tears shatter the illusion of control. Jesus delivered his own message of hope first through tears. This was no hand-scrawled note taped to a window.

He dignified the ceremony of grief by adding his own.

Tears require more out of us than a quick note.

Jesus' tears tell us that there is no God-ordained prescription to instantly alleviate heartache. There is only one way into our grief, and it begins by recognizing that

[12] John 11:35

our world has changed. Lazarus and Martha, Mary and Jesus would never be the same. They knew the absence of their friend and brother. Even though Lazarus walked out of the tomb, they were all changed.

We've heard grief described as a scar that fades with time, yet forever leaves its mark. Perhaps this idea resonates with some, but we have found that grief is more like a healing wound, tender to the touch, and always present beneath the surface. We have felt the fresh shock of long-ago grief, like finding your deceased friend's name in your address book. Suddenly we remember they are gone. Our losses are always present as tender tissues beneath the surface. In order to care for soul wounds, we need regular and intuitive dressing.

In the breaking open of old pain, we do not need to feel annoyed or disgusted with ourselves. This too is an invitation to begin with the first question: How will I go on?

What Tools Do We Have?

In Ray Bradbury's *Dandelion Wine*, Douglas Spaulding is playing statues for the last time with his best friend, John Huff. Tomorrow, John will move to another state. As Doug freezes for the final round, John socks Doug in the arm and says, "So long." Doug doesn't move, he waits until he knows no one is behind him and begins to run home. Once home, he tells himself over and over, "I'm mad, I'm angry, I hate him, I'm mad, I'm angry, I hate him." Slowly he reaches the top of the stairs, in the dark.

In darkness, we can easily feel alone in our pain. But, we are not left without resources. Just as the dark reveals the stars to guide the sailor to port, the dark nights of our souls can reveal the skills we already have for navigating our loss. We both found abilities latent within us that glided us into grieving well. In college, Jonalyn felt alienated and homesick. When she serendipitously found a baby grand piano to play, she visited it daily. Pounding through waltzes and nocturnes she began to feel release from her loneliness. Several years later, she again turned to playing piano to grieve and honor her mother-in-law. For Aubrie's grandmother's memorial, she arranged a version of "Amazing Grace" to sing at the burial site. Later on, when her dear friend died, creating a musical tribute again became the time-tested route for her grief.

Our loss is beyond our control; our grief is not. Mourning begins as we attempt to reconcile the pain we feel with the goodness we were sure existed. Before the pain began, we had places we smiled easily and let our hearts sing. It is with these same skills that we enter our grief. As Brené Brown writes in *The Gifts of Imperfection*, "I'm convinced there is a song, a dance, and a path to laughter for every human emotion."[13] Playing, singing, running, drawing, writing, gardening—what resources do each of us have?

Before you discovered this grief you had tools. Hold fast to these tools, use them, refashion them for another purpose. Apply them to consistently cultivate the reality of loss. None of us will lose the anchor of our souls.[14] He is on board even while we sail out into the depths.

[13] Brown, Brené, *The Gifts of Imperfection: Let Go of Who You Think You're Supposed to Be and Embrace Who You Are* (Minnesota: Hazelden, 2010), 118.

[14] Hebrews 6:19

Compass Checkpoint – 1

Listen to
"Fire and Rain" by James Taylor

Where are you now?
 This has happened:
 This will change:

1) What are your tools? Think of a loss from your childhood. Maybe a pet died or a good friend moved away. How did you respond? As a child, what did you do with your pain?

2) When you find yourself stressed out by work or a relationship, what do you do now, as an adult?

3) Have you ever explained a loss through journaling, writing a poem, dancing, sketching, playing a sport, or playing music? If you haven't tried one of these as an adult, did you ever write, draw, or play in the wake of a loss when you were a child? If so, revisit some in pictures or diaries. Hint: baby books are good places to look.

4) Reflect on the moments surrounding the loss you've experienced. Where were you when you found out? What did you see and hear, smell and feel when you received the news? Do you wish you had been more present? Use a creative tool that's helpful for you (writing, sharing with a friend, going for a walk).

Watch the film
The Descendants

1) How does each main character (Matt, Alexandria, Scottie, Sid) respond to Elizabeth King's coma? How are their tools for processing different?

2) Which character do you relate to the most?

3) Which characters are avoiding their grief? How do they rush past the moment?

Chapter 2
What Our Faith Can (and Cannot) Do

*We cannot beautify death. We may live with it and accept it,
but we cannot change its foul nature. The Apostle Paul spoke
of death as an enemy, "the last enemy to be destroyed." Death
is the enemy of God, of man made in God's image.*
— Joseph Bayly[15]

In the days of grief, our faith in a good God may clash
with our tangible loss. Jonalyn and Aubrie have both
felt that clash.

Jonalyn remembers her mobile phone ringing and
picking up to hear her husband's voice break as he said,
"Mom has flown to Jesus." His voice sounded serene as he
shared. He was in Florida. He watched her leave planet
earth. Jonalyn was about to teach a class of disrespectful
eighth graders. Hanging up the phone she heard a cluster
of junior high girls laughing at their own private joke.
Her only thought was, *How dare they! How dare anyone
laugh when her mother-in-law had died! How could God
allow people to be so wholly unaware? How could God take
Lois Ann, the one faithful parent left in her husband's family
tree?*

As Aubrie sat with a friend dying of breast cancer,
she often saw a positive warrior. Her battle-winning
language was so consistent, despite the circumstances of

---

[15] *The Last Thing We Talk About*, (Illinois: David C. Cook Publishing Co.:
1984), p15.

her dependency on others for her basic needs. One day
she asked Aubrie to listen to a special song. She made sure
to preface with, "This is not positive. And it's about God.
Just . . . warning you."

"Alright, alright," Aubrie smiled, "I can take it,"
reassuring her by pushing play. The lyrics of Sarah
McLachlan's "Dear God" flowed boldly. The injustice
that humans suffer, how little sense it all seems to make.
Was God even believable? When the song ended, Aubrie
turned to her friend and asked, "Do you feel this way?"
She stared right back, revealing for the first time the pain
behind her eyes. "Sometimes . . . sometimes, I just don't
understand."

Darkened Counsel

Pain may push us to ask new questions of our faith
because our faith is not peripheral or disconnected from
our loss. When faced with the changed world we may
want to try to neatly weave God into the pain. We may be
tempted to think God is testing us by adapting James 1:2-
4 to our loss.

Consider it pure joy, my brothers and sisters,
whenever you face trials of many kinds, because
you know that the testing of your faith produces
perseverance. Let perseverance finish its work so
that you may be mature and complete,
not lacking anything.

We've noticed it's very easy to use this verse on
someone in pain. When it has been quoted to us we felt
that God's words were being used against their purposes:
to interpret our pain away instead of grieve with us.

All losses can build perseverance in us, but not all losses mean God is schooling us until we get some new insight. For the biblical Job, his losses were a direct result of the Evil One's accusation, not God's doubt. To God, Job had nothing to prove. To Satan, Job had everything to prove. We must not mix up the voice of the Accuser with the voice of the Prince of Peace.

> *To God, Job had nothing to prove. To Satan, Job had everything to prove.*

Loss doesn't prove God's disappointment or his distance. Loss doesn't mean we're out of favor with God. Elijah and Elisha both served God faithfully as prophets of Israel. God gave Elijah a chariot of fire for his death day.[16] God permitted Elisha years of physical debilitation and sickness as he slowly approached death.[17] No commentary is made in our Scriptures about the apparent unequal treatment. Some of us will suffer longer and more than others. God wasn't closer to Elijah than Elisha. The trial Elisha endured doesn't prove he needed more faith than Elijah. Buddhism teaches that we, through karma, caused suffering. In the Scripture, we see how suffering doesn't simply land on the guilty, pain also falls on the innocent. The sacrificial lamb each year proves that the innocent suffer, again and again, for the sins of the guilty. As Adam and Eve's offspring pain follows each of us. Pain is not consistently a result of God's displeasure.

Our faith does not explain why we suffer, at least not

---

[16] 2 Kings 2:11
[17] 2 Kings 13:14

all the time. But we all grapple for a reason, sometimes if only to feel we have a hold on what's next, to feel we can predict the future. Giving a "why" to suffering feels like a quick route out of the pain. Remember the aftermath of the horror of Sandy Hook's shootings. Social media lit up with blame casting. Every person offered a solution, from gun control, to mental health databases, to arming schools. Some let themselves suffer with the parents of these victims. Few talked about the suffering of the shooter himself. We all wanted to explain.

We can prevent some suffering by taking simple safety measures, like wearing seat belts. But Jesus said, "In the world you will have tribulations," some suffering will hit our lives no matter how many insurance policies we buy, or how many risks we avoid.[18] The pain of losing a mother-in-law or a daughter is not the same as the pain of burning our hand on the stove. The latter is avoidable, but the former is not. Job teaches us that God does not answer the "Why?" But Job's friends insist they knew the "why" and God calls their words darkened counsel.[19]

Darkened counsel is so easy to give, but it compounds suffering. When Jonalyn received counsel in the week of grief after her mother-in-law's death, simple sounding sentences like "She's not suffering anymore," only darkened her suffering. Such an obvious line, she felt patronized. She wanted to retort, "That is not why I'm crying." She also endured close family members telling her, "You can get through this on your own; you don't need us to attend the funeral." The lack of support during her and Dale's grief meant Jonalyn flew to Florida alone,

---

[18] John 16:33
[19] Job 38:2

sat with her husband at his mother's wake and funeral, supported him as he spoke at her memorial, without a soul from her hometown and community sitting next to her.

So few want to let death inconvenience them enough to buy tickets, fly across the country, interrupt their schedules. So few can sit in silence when someone they love cries. But silence and presence are perhaps the best gifts. Sit quietly with someone who suffers and be God's arms and eyes even when others cannot feel his presence.[20]

TRUTH!

Let Your Faith Work

Job did not know the reason he suffered, but he suffered knowing God was near, with strength to save, even if the salvation felt tardy. Job models what loud suffering can look like—enduring, vocal suffering. As Job lay in the dust, he did not stop explaining to God and his friends all the injustice he endured. As James writes, "As you know, we count as blessed those who have persevered. You have heard of Job's perseverance and have seen what the Lord finally brought about. The Lord is full of compassion and mercy."[21]

Our faith means we can have the patience of Job, who waited on the Lord. It does not mean we automatically know the reasons for our suffering.

Just like Job, most of us have memories of God's compassionate ways to us. We all know times when the ways of God were clearer, when he showed us he would

[20] Psalm 145:18
[21] James 5:11

provide, or brought us a new friend or a spouse or a child just in time. But now, his faithfulness looks dried up.

Our faith in God means we bring Him into our suffering, just as we invited him into our joy. Jesus' last words on earth promised that he would not leave us to fend for ourselves.[22] He can walk with us into our doubt and fear. He comforted his followers with these words: "I have told you these things, so that in me you may have peace. In this world you will have trouble. But take heart! I have overcome the world."[23] He understands the grief, just as he is grieved over Lazarus' death while knowing death would be overcome with a resurrection in Bethany. Even when Jesus was in the Garden and wondered about the need for his own crucifixion, he brought God's mercy into his suffering.

Whenever a community pushes us to overcome grief to prove our faith, we might be tempted to lower our sails and rev up the engine. Why do this hard work of sailing through the storm when we have the power to muscle through it and pop out on the other side? But Jesus shows us another way. He never rushed others through their grief, so we invite you to notice where you need to be in your grief. Shelve the voices that are pushing you. Let your faith work with your grief rather than pushing you to finish up prematurely.

Let your faith work with your grief rather than pushing you to finish up prematurely.

[22] Matthew 28:20

[23] John 16:33

Who are you right now? See if you can allow God to collect the parts of yourself that have divided and reshape you in the present. This looks different for everyone. For example, to lose a parent means losing priceless pieces of your identity. New titles, like "orphan," may feel horrible right now. Begin by praying in this new normal, not inventing how you ought to be or feel. Let yourself be flustered, frustrated, focused, or broken. Bring these titles, not yet worn-in, to your relationship with God by following Checkpoint 2.

Compass Checkpoint – 2

Listen to
"I Have Not Seen This Day Before"
http://www.youtube.com/watch?v=r4Pn5IET30w

> Lyrics begin with:
> If I could I would break into flower.
> If I could I'd no longer be barren.
> This day is filling up my room,
> Is coming through my door.
> Oh I have not seen this day before.

1) How do I push my pain away? What do I do when I remember what I lost? Do I eat, do I workout, do I cry? How do I meet the pain in my life?

2) What makes me feel better? What makes me feel worse? At what time of day or the week do I feel better? Or worse?

3) Sometimes grief feels like a slow torture. Read Psalm 22, the words Jesus footnoted from the cross. If Jesus felt all that Psalm 22 communicates, what range of emotions did he experience during his crucifixion?

4) What are 8-10 feeling words (e.g. annoyed, alone, fragile, free, relieved) describing how my loss makes me feel today? No emotion is off limits.

5) Sometimes we have trouble receiving comfort when we think poorly of people who need comfort. Dig into that with these questions: When I have seen someone and want to comfort them, do I think of them as weak

or strong in their suffering? Does the idea of comfort embarrass or bother me?

6) Is there someone who comforts me better than others? Write this person's name down. What makes their comfort good?

Watch the film
Lars and the Real Girl

1) After Bianca's hospitalization, how do the ladies in the church make space for Lars' grief?

2) What questions do the women of the church ask Lars in his living room (the scene where they bring Lars casseroles and are each doing needlework)? What do they allow Lars to do?

3) How long does it take for Lars to grieve the loss of his mother?

4) What must Lars do to stop blaming himself for his mother's death?

5) When do you see a turning point in his own grief toward healing?

6) What do you learn about the love of God shown through a community?

Chapter 3
Learning the Language of Your Loss

Your absence has gone through me.
Like thread through a needle.
Everything I do is stitched with its color.
— M.S. Merwin[24]

Jonalyn once showed a family member a ring she had designed. It had taken upwards of a year and a bit of savings. As she held it out, the sapphire sparkling, the white gold begging for adoration, this family member was unimpressed. So she quickly slipped the ring back on her finger and tried to change the subject.

Grief is like that precious, time-costly ring, an expensive undertaking that few will thoroughly appreciate. Grieving well is costly. Energy you could have spent on friends or family must be spared. You have hard work ahead to learn a new language.

Grief means outwardly doing less in order to save the resources to vent, to journal, to take long walks, to cry, to stare off into space and think. To take up the utterly un-Western practice of doing less to learn more. It's no wonder Americans

> *Grief is neither dependable nor efficient, but it will make us more human.*

[24] "Separation" from *The Second Four Books of Poems* (Port Townsend, Washington: Copper Canyon Press, 1993

don't have time for it. Grief is neither dependable nor efficient, but it will make us more human.

Avoiding Grief

Grief is like tacking upwind while the waves surge over our sideboard. Sounds unpleasant and unnecessary, which is why many of us prefer to head below deck. Sailing into and through grief requires navigating the waves and the wind, but also navigating our own fear. We have both been tempted to avoid grief.

Dr. Alan Wolfelt's work as a grief and loss counselor identifies five avoidance patterns. We all have tendencies toward one of these patterns.

The **Postponer** keeps grief at arm's length, hoping to avoid the pain until it fades away. Grief is an unwanted visitor, never invited past the front step. Postponers may be perceived as doing better than expected or quickly recovering from a loss.

The **Displacer** avoids expressing grief by shifting to a less threatening alternative. Displacers are always looking for a scapegoat to blame. They might suddenly initiate arguments with a spouse or a coworker, or even start to despise themselves. Self-loathing is a sign of a Displacer hard at work.

The **Replacer** looks for a task, not to honor loss, but to keep busy. A replacer won't be busy organizing meaningful events, as much as avoiding pain by staying preoccupied. For example, Replacers eagerly work overtime in order to replace grief work with paid work. Or work takes the form of a project for a loved one, like starting family reunions or initiating a family foundation. Busyness helps Replacers steer clear of their own pain.[25]

The **Minimizer** might say, "I didn't really know them that well." Minimizers defer to rationalizing, attempting to prove that they were not impacted by their loss.

The **Somaticizer** will develop physical symptoms in an attempt to either gain attention or legitimize a need to be comforted. These symptoms are more severe than those regularly brought on by grief, such as chronic poor health (and obsession with such changes) that a physician will not be able to diagnose.

Seeing yourself in one of these patterns doesn't mean you're failing to grieve well or your boat has capsized. Avoiding grief is more like refusing to leave the dock. Finding avoidance in yourself will prepare you to know what you're working with and how to respond. Climbing back on deck, preparing to set sail will be costly, but not as costly as staying below. Any of these avoidance patterns have the potential to lead to depression, anxiety, restless thoughts, or sleep deprivation. To sail through grief, you must stay on deck.

Any of these avoidance patterns have the potential to lead to depression, anxiety, restless thoughts, or sleep deprivation.

[25] Distinct from the "Doer' discussed in Chapter 5, who uses activities to face grief.

Lists and Waves

In our experience, the most costly and rewarding requirement of grief is to allow ourselves to be exactly where we are, when we are. When we must cancel dinner plans because we're simply too fragile to buck up and keep our date, it costs more than a friend's disappointment; it costs our own disappointment in ourselves. We are forced to notice how we judge ourselves for not being able to "pull it together."

Pain calls us like a lover would, at inopportune moments— when we are busy at work, when we are entertaining friends, when we're in a crowded movie theater. And, like a lover, pain makes a mess of our plans. Grieving is never tidy. The pain stops us just when we need to run to the store to finish shopping in time for dinner. The tears spring to our eyes and we brush them back, almost ferociously, in an effort to keep the conversation rolling. Grief makes us lose our train of thought, but we press forward to finish the conversation.

> *Pain calls us like a lover would . . .*

Grieving does not work like a to-do list, simply because humans cannot work through pain so methodically. In every aspect of our fast-paced lives, we are trained to collect a to-do list, and then dutifully (and speedily) begin to check it off. Many grief books give the five states of grief,[26] simply laid out, which may lead to the assumption that grieving is simply a sequential to-do list.

---

[26] Kubler-Ross' five grief stages are widely known and often suggested for grievers.

Some grievers mistakenly assume that eventually all the boxes can be checked off and the grieving finished. Any step-by-step method to overcome pain might be helpful along the way, but grief promises no fast lane.

Fluidity and unpredictability are part of grief. Speed is not. Grief is much like the waves in the ocean; they suddenly wash over us.[27] Years after a death something very simple, like finding a hairbrush or receiving mail with our loved one's name, can make us feel a bubbling emotion or a physical surge similar to a panic attack. Jane Kenyon describes a wave of grief delivered to her while unpacking her friend's gravy boat. In "What Came to Me" she talks about something as small as a hard, brown dollop of gravy sitting on the porcelain lip.

Fluidity and unpredictability are part of grief. Speed is not.

> I grieved for you then
> as I never had before.[28]

Once we gear up for the slow work of grief, we may find some well-intentioned people more distracting than helpful. Speedy expectations of friends or our church community's "Christian" phrases can dishonor what we are facing. Well-meaning friends may approach with comments like "At least they are no longer suffering," "Isn't it about time [to move on]?"or "Isn't it beautiful—

---

[27] These bubbles are what grief experts call "STUG" for sudden, temporary upsurges of grief. Therese Rando (1993), *Treatment of Complicated Mourning*, (Champaign, IL: Research Press).

[28] Copyright Jan Kenyon http://www.poets.org/viewmedia.php/prmMID/19088

they are in eternity with Jesus!" We get wind through friends that acquaintances are wondering, "How is he doing with the loss?" which may be a veiled form of, "How long is he going to be upset about this?"

Within the comforting walls of the Church, we've stripped ourselves of a language for loss. What David and the psalmists spoke fluently, we have unlearned. We do not know how to sit with someone in his or her suffering without trying to fix it.

> *. . . we've stripped ourselves of a language for loss.*

A word to comforters: Provide the tissues within reach in case they need to use them—but do not pull the tissue out for them.[29] While watching their faces contort or flood with tears, just let them cry. Death is a horrible reality. If we are honest before our Lord and with ourselves, it hits us like a punch to the stomach, knocking the wind out of our bodies and leaving us doubled over in more confusion. Honor pain with your own steps into the pain.

We cannot begin to grieve if we are our own first critics. How much compassion do we have for ourselves when suffering? What about our friends? We cannot freely share our pain if every suffering statement finds a response in someone's curing, fixing attempts at comfort. We each must re-learn how to speak about and respond to loss.

When Jonalyn's son was two, he would re-tell any personal injury, drumming up an audience to live through the tragedy he just endured. "Do you

---

[29] Example given by Dr. Terry Martin, Hood College.

remember?" he would begin. "I bumped my head. Bam! Right here. Look, right here. Bang!" He replayed it for his parents, step by painful step.

If Jonalyn said, "But how do you feel now? Any better?" he would briefly nod only to explain it again. Prompting him to feel better was evidence to him that he wasn't fully understood. Any listener would then be subjected to another re-enactment. When a new person came to visit, he would claim this new audience to tell his story again. Two year olds are like their parents: they do not want curing comfort, they want caring comfort. They want attentive listeners who care to hear the details of their suffering.

Prompting him to feel better was evidence to him that he wasn't fully understood.

If we are in pain, we want someone skilled at our side. We don't want the distancing work of sympathy ("Oh, you poor thing!") or the rushing work of impatience ("Are you still grieving?"). We want the empathy of silence. All sufferers, from the biblical Job to our suffering Messiah, want comfort in the form of listening and tears, prayers and attentiveness.

To tell the stories of our lives we must become skilled in telling our pain. Even if our circle of friends treat our pain as alien, suffering proves we are human, that we belong to this blue planet. We recommend hunting for worthy audiences, for all good stories need an audience that can weep and laugh and let their eyes grow round in shock. We need to develop the ears of a focused audience and the re-telling enthusiasm of a two year old.

As we wade into the reality of what we feel, we'll find our entire bodies responding. Death always affects us holistically. We may feel disoriented or unable to concentrate on simple tasks. Sleep may feel like a haunting impossibility at times, or be our only option in moments of despair. It is normal to experience symptoms of sickness that range from wrenching stomach pain, regular headaches, or even a tightening of the chest. The inconsistencies of our body are more evidence that grief cannot be quantified or parceled out in one or two weeks of "bereavement leave" from work. Our body is evidence enough that we cannot simply "pull it together" over loss.

Our soul, the center of our beliefs, desires, choices, and emotions will be reacting to the loss. We may find ourselves compensating with our old patterns. The first time a song reminded Aubrie of her grandmother, she instinctively reached for her phone. She had all nine digits pressed before realizing, around the second ring, that her grandmother was no longer alive. She hung up overwhelmed and angry with herself for forgetting the most visceral and unforgettable pain of her death. It took Aubrie about five years before she stopped having these momentary trips out of life without her grandmother. Little by little, she began to feel more connected to her grandmother's absence. Instead of picking up the phone, she'd share the memory with another family member. Sometimes they'd even laugh over reminiscing.

We have also lost the pieces of ourselves that came alive in this connection and relationship.

When someone we love dies, our immediate connection to his or her space-filling presence is severed.

This emptiness may feel like disbelief, confusion, or preoccupying thoughts. Nothing seems to make sense. We feel like we've lost a piece of ourselves. And we have. We have also lost the pieces of ourselves that came alive in this connection and relationship. If Calvin, Grace, and Emma are friends and Emma dies, then all three lose. Grace loses not only Emma, but the way Calvin's face lights up over Emma's antics. And Calvin loses not just Emma, but Emma's way of getting Grace to try new things. C.S. Lewis describes this interdependent effect in *The Four Loves*.

> In each of my friends there is something that only some other friend can fully bring out. By myself I am not large enough to call the whole man into activity; I want other lights than my own to show all his facets.[30]

[handwritten margin note: Mary Dad + Justin/Kyle r JJ]

This realization may feel jarring and worrisome. Because every relationship and what it creates is unique, it will be uniquely missed. The brain forms memories in neurochemical train-tracks that leave imprints for retrieval. But the tracks are not permanent and the brain's storage is limited. Over time, the brain reacts to our inability to continue this retrieval process. We suddenly cannot remember what his voice sounded like, or the punch line in the story he always told. We experience a kind of chemical trauma. Grief adapts more like a cycle, changing every time we

Grief adapts more like a cycle, changing every time we experience a new "first."

[30] Lewis, C.S., *The Four Loves*, 61.

experience a new "first." We face our first Thanksgiving without Grandpa. The first time we forget what our sister's laugh sounded like. The first time we've had to change the oil in our car, because he always did that for us.

In Maria Howe's poem "The Gate," she describes the experience of her brother's death knocking her awake. The sharpness of the separation gives her the freedom to be just where she is, on her side of the divide, without him.

> I had no idea that the gate I would step through
> to finally enter this world
> would be the space my brother's body made.[31]

We have both found freedom in finding a language for our grief. But since expression will be customized to each of us individually, we want to provide exercises for everyone to find their own grief language. No feelings need to be held back or edited. David in the Psalms is a good model. He was a man after God's heart, and yet, no emotion was off-limits in his words to the heavens.

[31] onbeing.org/program/feature/the-gate-by-marie-howe/5316

Compass Checkpoint – 3

Listen to
Your Language of Grief

Rebuild your language of loss by reading Psalm 30:7b-10 and Psalm 109. Is there a line you wish you could say?

1) What are some firsts you have faced or are anxious about facing?

2) Grieve actively through directing letters or journals to the person who has died or is gone.

3) Designate a period of time just for mourning and remembering. How would you most like to honor this person?

4) Read or write a poem to express your grief. Here is one to get your started:

Allow Me to Demonstrate You
by Amy Kaneko

with my best handwriting

I fill in your blanks
until I realize
there aren't enough blanks
in this blankety world
to articulate you.

so instead I draw.
I press and shift

charcoal lines onto paper
only to find that
even the best shading
can't do the moment
between purple and blue any justice.

so then I sing.
I hit the low notes for your heavy
and I rock-climb highs for your light
but my voice catches
whenever I try to sing
the notes you leave me
in the bathroom

when a sound echoes into a cave
there's no saying how many
chambers bounce back those vibrations

still, that doesn't stymie the sound.

5) Watch a movie or listen to a song that bubbles up memories for you. Here are three suggestions: *Life is Beautiful, Charlotte's Web, Of Gods and Men*.

Chapter 4
Your Path Through Grief

What is central is the recognition that human beings . . . are likely to respond to important losses in their lives with their whole selves, not just with some narrowly defined aspect of their humanity. Failure to describe grief in a holistic way dismisses and devalues its richness and breadth.
— Charles Corr[32]

Your mother dies and you want to start training for a marathon? Normal. Your mother dies and you stop going to church and stay home for months? Normal. You forget your son's birthday? Normal. You sleep for 10 hours a night one week and spend the next with insomnia? Normal. You miss an appointment and forget to fill the gas tank? Normal. Nearly all reactions to grieving are normal.[33]

One woman, Margaret, wrote about a breakdown she had one month after her father's death.

> Yesterday I had a bit of a breakdown. We were on the golf course and everyone kept trying to get me to play and even though I really didn't want to, they

---

[32] Corr, C. (1998). "Enhancing the concept of disenfranchised grief." *Omega: The Journal of Death and Dying*, 38, p.13.

[33] An important distinction: the depressive symptoms that accompany grief are normal. Grief can develop into depression, but it is not depression. Dr. Martin explains, "In grief, the world looks poor and empty, in depression the world feels poor and empty." If you are experiencing chronic (lingering) thoughts of suicide or worthlessness, please seek help from a professional.

guilted me into it. And it was not so great, since golf is all about focus and every time I went to swing the only thing I could think of was my dad; of how he loved the game and how he'd always try to teach us and how I was never any good even though I always wanted to impress him.

I stood there, hovering over that tiny, dimpled white ball; I just wanted to make one good shot. Just one. But I couldn't feel him and I couldn't hit a thing and I just kept swinging and swinging and hitting nothing but air . . . and that's when I started to cry. And once I started I couldn't stop and I just kept getting more upset.

It was an ugly and embarrassing cycle, especially since they all thought I was crying because I was frustrated at not being able to hit the ball. I tried to explain through gasps and sobs but all I got out was "My dad . . ."

So then everyone started cooing and didn't know what to do so I felt like such an emotional freak show. I mean, I cry like that often enough these

I don't want to be fussed over.

days, I just try not to show it or involve other people. I don't want to be fussed over. I want someone to bring him back for five minutes so I can say what I need to say and get all these horrible uncertainties off my chest.

We grieve in unexpected ways that cannot be compared with those around us. It is too easy for

Margaret to compare herself to her sister who plays golf without a breakdown. It is too easy for us to judge her sister as cold-hearted or in denial.

Comparing grief, especially between spouses or siblings, will only serve to muffle the capacity to hear the rhythm of grief. And it will likely grow resentment. When a mother dies, each sibling will fumble through the loss differently. One sister may seem unaffected *(She didn't take any days off work!)* compared with another who plummets into depressive feelings. Her appearance of "keeping it together" only means she has taken another path through grief.

Not just every person, but every grief, is different. Any mother of several children knows that births are not all the same. Each child grows and comes into the world differently. So it is with death. Each person we lose affects us uniquely. We may have experienced multiple deaths, even within a short period of time, but we cannot know how we will grieve the next death.

Grieving isn't like the skill of riding a bike; it's more like the skill of sailing. Skilled sailors know what to do when the skies turn slate, when the wind stings their cheeks. But even the most seasoned sailor knows it is impossible to cut the same path through the ocean twice. The paths through the seas, and our paths through grief change. In this way, we cannot become so good at grief that the process becomes easy. Every line we take through the sea of grief is both rewarding and

> *Every line we take through the sea of grief is both rewarding and painful.*

painful. We may recognize some harbors and currents, the same stars and blue sky, but our route cannot be repeated.

Gender, background, and vocation cannot foretell the path of grief. Women are not more natural *feelers*, nor men *doers*. Extensive Bible knowledge cannot accelerate grief, nor can it be detained by meager

The pastor does not grieve better than the plumber.

knowledge. The pastor does not grieve better than the plumber. Extroverts will not grieve faster than introverts.

Though we cannot be sure of how we will grieve, it may help to know a few different styles of grieving. Two grief experts from the Association of Death Educators and Counselors, Drs. Kenneth Doka and Terry Martin, explain two styles. We will call them Feelers and Doers.[34] And despite myths to the contrary, both grieving styles are equally helpful. Both Feelers and Doers bring wise tools to the task of grieving. Even more, the differences between Feelers and Doers complement each other. Although most grievers are in reality "blended grievers," you will probably find yourself landing more to one side of the continuum than the other.

When the biblical King David lost his first son, he acted as a Doer—he washed his face, anointed his head, worshipped God, and prepared to take on his duties. He ate and drank and sustained himself for work.[35] But

[34] Doka and Martin use the terms intuitive and instrumental grievers. To simplify the basic intentions of each term, we've called them Feelers and Doers.

[35] 2 Samuel 12:16-23

before his son died, David was a Feeler; he wept and refused food. He lay on the ground all night begging God to spare his son. David focused on his pain before God. He mourned. David blended his grief with both feeling and doing.

Laura had a painful relationship with her dad. She was separated from him most of her life, and his drug addiction made her more of a regular caregiver than a daughter. When he died, Laura was thinking all the same things her siblings were expressing. Since Doers find active sharing exhausting and sometimes unnecessary, Laura struggled to match her siblings' sad emotions. She mostly felt . . . relief. As Laura explained,

> In a way, as horrible as this might sound to some people, his death made me have a dad again, and our relationship so much stronger. All the anger, stress, worry, and animosity was gone, and at the end it was just a girl who loved her dad regardless of how he lived his life.

To Laura's siblings, who were Feelers, it would have been easy to think Laura was "in denial" or impervious to pain. Doers are the kind of people who get dragged to support groups or find themselves accused of being cold and aloof. For Doers, grief is largely an intellectual experience; you might even call them "Doer-Thinkers." Since most of their energy is channeled towards problem finding and solving, Doers often experience more confusion and disorientation than

Doers often experience more confusion and disorientation than Feelers.

Feelers.

Laura no longer had to play the part of the dutiful daughter, tending to the needs of everyone else who felt threatened by her father's illness. In the beginning, she didn't cry. Pieces she thought were resolved would bubble up out of nowhere. She found that her grief process began in *doing* different things rather than *feeling* different things. She started planning and saving for her future. She decided to go back to school, taking care of herself with the same energy she had devoted to her father. Later the same year, Laura's dog died, allowing her to revisit her father's death with additional perspective. This time her experience was full of sadness. For Laura, losing her dog supplied the emotional vocabulary to feel her father's death.

Feelers haven't really *felt* grief unless they have expressed it externally. Feelers might feel comfortable spilling emotions to close friends rather than organizing a memorial service. They will not always be able to get the kids ready for school without breaking into a torrent of tears.

Ryan expected to fall apart when he lost his mother, but his uncle gave him the advice: "Be strong for your mom." Suddenly, Ryan found that he couldn't cry naturally. Later, when his childhood teacher died of a rare form of cancer, he attended the memorial. He found that the simple act of standing in the church alongside his community moved him deeply. He found himself sobbing. As a Feeler, tears helped Ryan move into his grief. Later, he wrote a song to fill in the gaps between his experience and his feelings.

Once again, people cannot anticipate if they will be a Doer of a Feeler. As an enthusiastic extrovert, Jonalyn expected that her dog's death would push her to call friends and talk and story-tell. But when Lady Lucia died, she did not call anyone. She wanted to do something tangible. She tucked her son into the baby carrier and dug a grave through frozen earth. She planned a poem to read at Lucy's gravesite. And she wrote more than usual. Grief surprised her.

Psychiatrist and death studies pioneer, Elizabeth Kubler-Ross, gives another model of grief. The five stages appear, at first, deceptively simple: denial, anger, bargaining, depression, and acceptance. These stages put language to emotions. For example, if a woman finds herself repeatedly writing angry letters to the hospital's medical staff, she can recognize that anger is a valid emotion to be feeling after her loss. Or when you discover your friend's grief is causing them to be late or miss work, since they cannot get out of bed in the mornings, you can recognize grief's stage of depression and not rush for clinical help.

However useful these stages have become, Kubler-Ross did not intend to prescript a regular, stage-like progression. Kubler-Ross did not want people to march through these stages, checking them off as completed.

Death reveals new things in each individual that no model or list of steps can anticipate. Unfortunately, American culture is driven to put pain to rest, to normalize grief with unhelpful questions, like, "What stage am I in?" or "What stage am I missing?" Grief isn't a monopoly board with a "GO" square. Grief doesn't have

American culture is driven to put pain to rest . . .

clear or definitive stops and starts. Kubler-Ross' stages are phases that one may or may not experience, and not necessarily in a prescribed order.

Dr. William Worden, a leading researcher in the field of grief and bereavement, offers four tasks that can come in any order. Worden's work can help solidify and even replace Kubler-Ross' five stages with four tasks of mourning:

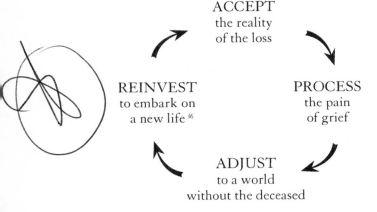

ACCEPT
the reality
of the loss

PROCESS
the pain
of grief

ADJUST
to a world
without the deceased

REINVEST
to embark on
a new life [36]

We highly recommend this model because it honors the physical and emotional work of grief, but doesn't force a sequential order. [37]

When the biblical Naomi loses her husband and both her sons, she <u>adjusts</u> to her new life by leaving Moab. [38] As Naomi begins the journey back to Bethlehem, she <u>accepts</u>

[36] By finding an enduring connection with the deceased so you can withdraw from grief to embark in a new life.

[37] While the four tasks are not intended to be taken in order, Worden notes that the order is suggested based on each task's definition. (For example, one cannot experience the pain of a loss until they accept that the loss has happened.)

[38] Ruth 1:5-6

that she is alone, urging her daughters-in-law to reinvest with their Moabite families and possibly new husbands.[39] Naomi is still <u>processing</u> her loss when she arrives, asking her Bethlehem friends to call her "Mara," which means bitter.[40] She is still <u>processing</u> the emptiness she feels. Naomi isn't ready to <u>reinvest</u>; she cannot even provide for her and Ruth's basic needs. It is Ruth's idea to find food for them from a relative.[41] Not until Ruth finds favor with Boaz does Naomi's shrewd <u>reinvestment</u> return with full force.[42] When Ruth is ready for her daughter-in-law to love another man, she begins <u>reinvesting</u> in future generations.[43]

We appreciate how Worden's tasks honor the hard work of grief. Each of Worden's tasks must be faced at some point in our journey. If a task is avoided, it will only pop up again around another bend. And each task will look different for each person and for each grief.

Jenna's family handed her the decision to remove their father from the ventilator. "It doesn't get more real than that," she said. "He was there one minute, and then he was . . . gone." From the beginning, Jenna <u>accepted</u> the reality of her loss. <u>Processing</u> the pain of her grief was not something she gave herself permission to do right away, not until the first time she changed a flat tire without the help of her dad. Getting out the jack to hoist the car on her own was <u>adjusting</u> to the world without her father. Once she realized the gap he left, she was <u>able</u> to experience the ache of <u>processing</u>. She gave herself one

[39] Ruth 1:8-15
[40] Ruth 1:20-21
[41] Ruth 2:2-3
[42] Ruth 3:1-4
[43] Ruth 4:16-21

hour every day to listen to the grief and follow it. Even if that meant she lost control and sobbed for an hour, she released control. She would drive to the beach nearby and sit in her car, sobbing and crying out in anger to God. She did this until she didn't have to anymore. It took her six months to process—and even two years later when she feels pieces bubble up, she gives herself that permission again. Jenna is presently working through reinvesting, discovering things like learning to run and volunteering at her daughter's school. These are new places to pour time, energy, and love.

When Jonalyn lost her mother-in-law, Lois Ann, attending her wake helped her accept this loss. But, it took nearly a year before she and her husband had the energy to trek across the country and wade through Lois' belongings. Being in Lois's home without her active presence forced Jonalyn to begin processing the pain. The process continued when they drove many of Lois' belongings 3,000 miles home to Los Angeles. These "linking objects"[44] were very precious in the years after her death. Jonalyn and her husband wanted to prize the things Lois prized. To break a figurine or scratch a table was an affront to Lois and to their memory. When Jonalyn's son was born six years later, she felt she needed to further adjust to Lois' absence. Lois would never know her grandson.

When they built their first home, Jonalyn and her husband began to sort through and give away many of Lois' belongings. They found they could honor her by refusing to have a possessive-driven memory of her life. They now focus on three treasured items: an heirloom

---

[44] Dr. J. William Worden's concept

rocking chair, Lois' watercolors, and her letters to each of them. They began task four, reinvesting emotional energy, but it took nine years to reach that point.

When Aubrie was fourteen years old, her grandparents died within several months of each other. Aubrie and her father took on the excruciating task of combing through their belongings. She could not wrap her mind around their absence until she processed that their lives had been reduced to piles: clothing to give or throw away, untouched bath products, and kitchen items. The piles of newspaper clippings affected Aubrie most viscerally, simply because they were so meaningless to her. Aubrie kept all the clippings. Wouldn't tossing them away into the garage be tossing away pieces of meaning for her grandparents? Adjusting was difficult. Every piece was a memory inside Aubrie. Without these things, would she forget who they were, who she was?

Perhaps you've felt the same, to leave a bedroom untouched, mail unopened on the counter, empty chairs at the table. Processing often happens by bringing back the sights, words, and smells of loved ones.

Many years later, Aubrie can see that holding onto newspaper clippings temporarily helped her process the pain of no longer having her grandparents. The newspapers helped her recount their stories even to herself. But these clippings were not something she held on to forever. Instead, she decided to keep only three, laminating them. Today, she reinvests them as bookmarks for her favorite books. Every time she sees them, she can pause and remember. Without carrying the weight of those boxes of clippings, Aubrie was freed up to see their simple beauty, chosen with purpose by someone she loves.

Compass Checkpoint – 4

Listen to
"Hush Little Heart" by Daena Jay

So much of any loss experience leaves us feeling prematurely pruned. This song captures the tension between knowing life has changed and then speaking the truth of that change to our own hearts.

Lyrics begin with, "Birds fly away when the weather changes, why can't we do the same?"

Grief Story
1) Imagine that grief is like a maze with multiple paths, what adjectives would you use to describe the path you are on right now? Is it smooth or bumpy, rocky or sandy, cloudy or sunny, foggy or cold? Night or day? Full moon or no moon? If you can, draw, sketch, paint, or make a collage of your grief path.

2) Are you more a Feeler or a Doer-Thinker in your grief? Does this surprise you?

3) If you're a Feeler, who are the people you can call and talk about your feelings with? If you're a Doer, write down three things you've done after a loss that have helped you.

4) Have you found yourself comparing your grief to someone else? Were they a Doer or a Feeler?

5) Who has given you freedom to grieve in your unique way? Write down their name and what they did to free you.

6) List some "linking objects" that you own.

7) Grief is a time when nothing seems to fit together. Give yourself the permission and freedom to pay attention to what makes sense. If you crave a structure, make yourself a few lists and tackle them piece-by-piece. We recommend you consider categorizing these types of items:

    a. What's important but not urgent (ex: how to interact with your mother-in-law now that your husband is gone)

    b. What's important and urgent (ex: signing legal documents)

    c. What's urgent but not important (ex: it's time to change oil in your car)[45]

Watch the film
Away From Her

Losses can sometimes feel ambiguous. Perhaps someone you love has not yet died, but pieces of them, and likewise of your relationship, have begun to disappear. You may be taking on the role of a caregiver. The grief that bubbles up in these sorts of losses is referred to as "anticipatory" grief, and it is filled with many of the same hurdles as the other losses we've discussed so far.

Alzheimer's Disease is one loss that is gradual and multidimensional. It is the subject of *Away From Her*. Watch it first and then work through these questions.

1) As Fiona describes in the film, she is "going, but not gone." Her mind is "like a series of circuit breakers in a large house flipping off one by one." How have

---

[45] Dr. Terry Martin's distinctions

you noticed and accommodated the changes that have happened in your life since your grieving began? Have some changes been slower and others instantaneous? What is harder for you to face?

2) Fiona reads about what her husband will experience as her disease progresses. "The caregiver must preside over the degeneration of someone he or she loves very much. They must do this for years and years, with the news always getting worse (and never better), and must somehow learn to smile through it all." What is most challenging about tending to the needs of another?

3) Fiona describes her memories as they decline, "If I let it go, I will only hit it harder when I bump into it again." Have you had moments in grief where you've preferred to hang on rather than acknowledge the pain of your reality? Journal about the things you struggle to accept in your new reality. Allow yourself to be angry, upset, confused . . . whatever you are feeling. Pray that the Lord will meet you there.

Chapter 5
Mourning with Friends

*It is better to go to a house of mourning
than to go to a house of feasting,
for death is the destiny of everyone;
the living should take this to heart.*
— Solomon, Ecclesiastes 7:2

The person who touches us in our pain—a hand on our shoulder, a carefully written card, a moment of catching and holding our eyes—plays a magnificent supporting role. They must know how to touch with care, because the right kind of touch can ease even the worst suffering.

Isolated suffering is, perhaps, the worst kind. To keep from solitary pain, we must learn how to touch one another when our bodies and souls are most weak. As Soulation writer, Kelsey Vandeventer, wrote, "Could it be that we must touch each other in our discomfort and great weakness, especially as we lay dying, in order to remember that we are all sacred dust, need and bound for death?"

We can be near others even if we don't understand their personal journey. Parts of our grief journey will feel lonely, as no one can truly walk in our shoes. But, our

It can be dangerous to claim total sovereignty of our grief.

stubborn independence can turn our grief into a personal martyrdom, proof of our incredible reservoir of personal strength. This ownership might feel empowering, but it can be dangerous to claim total sovereignty of our grief. Our independence can actually keep our friends away.

When Jonalyn processed the pain of her broken engagement, she soldiered on through her finals with more willpower than normal. But one night, she broke. Her roommates all gathered around her while she unraveled her pain on her bed. They held her hands and feet and let her sob and question and rail. They were with her in her dark night of the soul and never once made her feel pathetic for being so undone. But they could not have rallied for her unless they had seen her need for a cheering section.

The communal nature of grief is something that comes instinctively to many cultures and traditions, yet it is not always the case for Americans. In place of dropped-off casseroles and endless bereavement cards, Judaism offers a practice called shiva, a time to shelter and uplift the grieving. It may seem reminiscent of the way biblical heroes, like Jacob, mourned.[46] For faithful Jews, death means every normal activity ought to halt.

The *shiva* is a seven-day period of pause for those directly affected by a death. The Jewish community literally comes home to the bereaved. Even during the burial preparations, a community from the synagogue will take over

For faithful Jews, death means every normal activity ought to halt.

[46] Genesis 37:34-35

the role of planning. Every beautiful detail, from making the casket to washing the body, is done with and by the community. The meal of consolation, which traditionally comes immediately after the funeral, provides nourishment for the body and soul of the griever. Round foods comprise the meal, to remind the bereaved how they are surrounded in their neediness. Prayer services are even relocated to the home of those grieving. This time is reserved to focus on the death.

Through *shiva*, the community creates structure as the bereaved walk into uncertainty. The community acts like captains, charting the course so the grieving can hold onto the side of the ship. As they grip the rails, they know no matter how they feel, someone else is steering them through the waves.

When self-care is most difficult, others will step in and make a way. Family sits together, sometimes on the floor to signify the lowliness of their spirit. Personal tasks like bathing or shaving are not observed. During shiva, grieving family members refuse entertainment, movies, the opera, attending parties, and eating out. Sometimes the family even covers mirrors, ignoring their appearance.

How can it be that the immediate family members are able to focus on nothing but their loved one for one week? The friends in their community provide meals during this time and each mourner paces each visit. The expectation is that the one who is mourning will initiate conversation if and when they need to do so, and any need until that point is met with simple companionship. The presence of a friend who refuses to speak into our grief until we initiate the conversation sounds to us like balm on a wound: the faithfulness of interested, patient, silent friends. May this be a picture of care that all of us yearn to give.

How can we take these aspects of surrounded care for one another into our Christian reality? When Aubrie's friend Leanna died, her closest friends wanted to be with one another, but they needed a context. They planned a dinner party at the home of Leanna's husband, bringing along a famous dish she'd certainly have made, and simply enjoyed being with each other. In the community they made, the unbearable and unspeakable walls came down. They were able to check in with each other, asking

> *In the community they made, the unbearable and unspeakable walls came down.*

the hard questions and accepting whatever answers came to the surface. They shared pieces of Leanna in their lives. Fear dissipated as story after story was shared about the woman whose laugher and antics commanded the attention of a whole room. By setting time apart to remember together, they found ample opportunities to express emotions and honor Leanna's life.

The ideas in Jewish *shiva* are biblically sound. Remember how Esther and Mordecai alter their clothing, wearing sackcloth and ashes to signify their grief?[47] David also, upon learning he will lose his son, refuses to eat and spends time praying and weeping.[48] We can easily imagine mirrors and showers were furthest from David's mind during this time. When Jacob learns he has lost his

[47] Esther 4:1-3
[48] 2 Samuel 12:17

favorite son, Joseph, he rips his clothes, wears sackcloth and ashes (not very comfortable or clean), and mourns for many days. In the words of Genesis, he "refuses to be comforted."[49]

Last time Jonalyn grieved deeply she found out who her closest friends were. They were the ones who had a kind of care that moved deeper than words, a kind of care that was simply quiet and present. They inspired her to vow that in the future she would be that presence for her friends.

To create *shiva* for those we love, we can begin by writing an email or making a call, opening up space to develop a vocabulary for grief. We can get together with the purpose of honoring the loss even (or especially) months or years after the death. We can invite others intentionally into our time of grief, asking them to cover for us while we fall apart. When someone experiences a loss, call after the first flood of meals, maybe on the first month or first holiday after the loss. Remembering when most have forgotten is what friends take time to do.

so much heart

We need the witness of another to navigate our own growth and healing. Every Father's Day, Aubrie calls the friend who lost her dad years ago. By remembering, Aubrie integrates her friend's benchmarks into her own life. She will see if her friend has grown more alive this year, or confirm that a trip to the movie theater in honor of her movie-buff dad sounds like a wonderful tribute. She can grant permission to grow and invite another perspective on her journey. A simple phone call can say, "Hey, I see you. It's so hard. And somehow you live on."

[49] Genesis 37:34-35

When Jonalyn watched her housemates tiptoe around the grief of her broken engagement, she felt glad for their silent, continued life. Final exams still rolled forward, as did Christmas break and New Year's. Housemates laughed over failed blind dates and she could listen in silence, wondering if her life wouldn't always feel so stuck. Back home on break, Jonalyn considered new possibilities, like graduate school or an internship in D.C. In the first few weeks of this loss, she felt bolder about seizing opportunities. She took chances and vacations with new friends. She bought a map of the world to symbolize how much was open to her. She pinned it above her bunk where she and her roommates could see despair turning into hope.

Family and friends are first to rally around a griever for the fresh embers of pain. But eventually the support becomes sparse and sometimes withdrawn. It seems the deeper into the journey we go, the more alone we become.

It seems the deeper into the journey we go, the more alone we become.

Grief therapist Dr. Catherine Saunders explains the need for connection in grief. Saunders suggests that we hoard the love and care we receive in the beginning of our grief, as a way to prepare for the leaner months. This hoarding is not greedy as much as it is wise, like an ant preparing for the winter.[50] We can create a storehouse of memories taken from all the early, enthusiastic support. The storehouse can look like a journal, or a series of pictures of the flowers, cards, or food we received during the first fresh weeks of our loss. We may not have time to

---

[50] Proverbs 6:6-8

note them, but we can snap pictures for later. This is one reason written cards are so valuable. They're tangible signposts to be saved. It's another reason to wait a few weeks or even a month to write a condolence card. A "tardy" card will arrive in a leaner time of comfort. Israel stockpiled their memories too, like stacking stones of remembrance to look back and see the Lord's goodness in preserving them.[51]

We can create a storehouse of memories taken from all the early, enthusiastic support.

You can also store up comfort by caring for yourself in ways you know you would tend to your friends. If you know you have weeks ahead on the open seas, you'll buy more and rest longer. For instance, you can give yourself permission to enjoy a movie marathon you've been putting off, a spa treatment you've never had, or a special restaurant with friends. You can write out Scripture and your favorite quotes and put them in places where you know you'll see them at next month's anniversary. You can create a scrapbook, photo album, or blog to preserve encouragement for yourself when you need it most. Storing up comfort is a discipline in remembering your weakness. You are not able to sustain yourself. But somehow, even in that neediness, Jesus says you are blessed, "Blessed are the poor in spirit for theirs is the kingdom of heaven."[52]

To learn to do anything new, from grieving to sailing, you need guides who have gone before. When Jonalyn and her husband bought their small sailboat, they

---

[51] Joshua 4:1-7
[52] Matthew 5:3

practiced on their local lake before they felt ready to sail on the larger bodies with the big boats.

They found themselves delighted to pull next to a large clipper and ask a few questions. It was a relief to see other, larger ships stalled in the windless zones too. If you're stuck in the questions of grief, bring these to others who have sailed before you. You will know it in their looks. Ask them how they faced the deaths in their life. You will find those who grieved well ready to share what brought them through the storms.

In these doldrums, refuse to only notice your own ship. Let your eyes light on the ships around you who are perhaps three leagues ahead, whose sails suddenly fill. Their pitch and speed promise the wind will pick up. You will sail through.

Compass Checkpoint - 5

Listen to
"Timshel" by Mumford and Sons
http://www.youtube.com/watch?v=kl-VCHzS1So

Lyrics include
And death is at your doorstep
And it will steal your innocence.
But it will not steal your substance.

1) In the opening quote from Ecclesiastes, Solomon writes, "by sadness of face the heart is made glad." What do you think that means?

2) When have you allowed someone to meet you in your need? Was that a positive or negative or a mixed experience for you?

3) Imagine how you could invite others to help you make a way in your grief. Who are the safe friends you could ask for a few extra meals, babysitting, company?

4) Invite someone in your life who can honor your loss. Do something with them that gives you space to talk about the person you lost, the good and the bad. Invite your friend to commemorate your lost one by something meaningful such as:
    ~ taking a drive or trip they would have loved
    ~ making and sharing a meal in their honor
    ~ visiting their burial plot with flowers, a prayer, or poem
    ~ supporting you as you cut your hair
    ~ buying a piece of jewelry, clothing, or furniture to remember
    ~ reading a book or watching a movie they valued

5) Proverbs 20:27 says "The human spirit is the lamp of the Lord that sheds light on one's inmost being." Even today, this verse guides Jewish mourners as they light a candle in memorial. As we are all made in God's image, so the spark of the candle reminds us that there is a lamp of God in all of us. Light a candle and watch how it flickers. Reflect on the light your loved one brought to the world.

Watch the film
We Bought a Zoo

1) Benjamin has trouble going anywhere or seeing any "trigger" that will remind him of his wife. He eventually discovers that he "can't get away" from his memories. He must find a way to integrate the memories and legacy of his wife. He gives his memories fresh eyes and new meaning by telling his children the stories he was pushing away. Have you avoided potential spaces and places of memories? Imagine telling a story about your loved one to a child. How would it go?

2) Benjamin's brother warns him not to become a reclusive griever, telling him to not give up on "human interactions" because he will find himself "missing people and sunlight." Because of the state of his grief, he's wise to direct Benjamin to community—but this progression cannot be forced. For some grievers, just allowing themselves to go to the grocery store for a half hour every day, taking a walk around the block, sitting on a bench for a few minutes, or chatting with the mailman might be ways to ease back into the rhythm of everyday life. How can you begin to revisit community in a way the makes sense for you?

3) Seven-year-old Rosie wakes to noisy neighbors. When she and her dad, Benjamin, open the curtains and look outside they see a party in full swing. Rosie says, "Their happy is too loud." It can be painful to feel isolated in our shifting world while the rest of life continues on without notice. Have you felt flustered or stunted by the "happy" in others during the dark and painful places of your own grief? Journal one of those times.

4) "Go ahead and travel the stages of grief, but stop before zebras are involved." Benjamin's brother cautions him against potentially hasty decisions and literal zebras. There may be times in your grieving when you find yourself ready to start such a (seemingly) crazy adventure. It may be the last thing you could ever imagine. Have you experienced this desire? What has been terrifying or foolhardy about this? Has there been any beauty behind the crazy?

Chapter 6
Reaching Shore

Sorrow ... knows its way
And will find the right time
To pull and pull the rope of grief
Until that coiled hill of tears
Has reduced to its last drop.
— "For Grief," John O'Donohue[53]

W hen birthdays and vacations, work and play seem to be moving on, a grieving person can feel stuck. How do we live well and grieve well at the same time? There will come a time when we are ready to move forward. For some, moving on seems unbelievable, as Tom Hanks' character, Sam, admits in *Sleepless in Seattle*.

> **Dr. Marcia Fieldstone**: People who truly loved once are far more likely to love again. Sam, do you think there's someone out there you could love as much as your wife?
>
> **Sam Baldwin**: Well, Dr. Marcia Fieldstone, that's hard to imagine.
>
> **Dr. Marcia Fieldstone**: What are you going to do?
>
> **Sam Baldwin**: Well, I'm gonna get out of bed every morning ... breathe in and out all day long. Then,

---

53 *To Bless the Space Between Us: A Book of Blessings* (New York: Doubleday, 2008) 118.

after awhile I won't have to remind myself to get out of bed every morning and breathe in and out . . . and then after awhile, I won't have to think about how I had it great and perfect for awhile.[54]

After awhile, we stop having to remind ourselves to keep going. We've been sailing in choppy seas, we're used to losing our stomachs and cresting waves to fall into a valley. The sails are whipping us, the boom is swaying, and we can merely hold on. Our friends excuse us from returning their phone calls; hopefully we aren't expected to be as present at church or work. All our emotions can be channeled into remembering who or what we lost. But this doesn't continue forever.

Suddenly, we catch a new smell in the air, tangy mixed with earth, the sweetness of leaves and grass. Land is ahead. We start noticing the waves are smoothing, that we want to get off the boat and try our land legs. We remember we like the stability of land.

The acute pains of grief will not remain as steady. The day will come when a task nearly unthinkable, such as rearranging a bedroom or cleaning out a desk drawer, will be the one thing that seems necessary in order to move forward. Charting a course for land and leaving the seas of grief is best begun with safe family or friends, coming together to find creative ways to reassemble our lives.

The day will come when a task nearly unthinkable . . .

In the film, *Rabbit Hole*, Becca and her mother

[54] *Sleepless in Seattle*. Dir. Nora Ephron. Tristar Pictures, 1993.

discuss this process. A year has passed since the death of Becca's child. They pack up all the contents of her son's vacant room, wading through and sorting which toys and clothing will be kept and stored. Finishing the last box, Becca steps back and surveys the looming pile.

. . . will be the one thing that seems necessary in order to move forward.

"Does it ever go away?" Becca asks her mother.

"No . . . It changes though. The weight of it, I guess. At some point it becomes bearable. It turns into something that you can crawl out from under and carry around like a brick in your pocket. And you even forget it for awhile, but then you reach in, for whatever reason, and there it is. 'Oh, right. That.' Which could be awful. But not all the time. It's kind of . . . not that you like it exactly, but it's what you've got instead of your son. So you carry it around. And it doesn't go away. Which is . . . fine. Actually."

The land we watch grow larger is not the same as the land we left. We are not the same. We carry new weight as we disembark. We will have sea legs that will feel like we are rising and falling, even in stable places.

When are we really ready to get out of the boat of grief? When we are able to do things that seemed impossible, like talk about our loss without breaking down, feel thankful for something beautiful, find energy to host Christmas again, or contribute to the loss of someone else in a meaningful way. After all, we've lived it and gained some wisdom.

Reuniting the fluidity of sailing with the firmness of

land isn't as graceful as we might imagine it to be. The peace of swaying boat dissipates as we lower the sail, lock the oars, and maneuver to line up with the dock. We're often forced to wade a bit, get wet, and hold the boat at awkward angles. Land that looked so good is not unforgivingly stable.

Living well, after a loss, can often feel just as awkward. We don't know how to return to our duties while remaining faithful to the one we lost. We have one foot on the quaking boat and one foot on the dock. Returning to regular tasks, getting out of bed and going to work, and working on homework with our children, can feel alternatively like a relief and betrayal. We must end up integrating slowly. We breathe in, we breathe out. We pack the kid's lunches and include a candy. We celebrate life. We care for ourselves.

And as we celebrate small things we may face the pangs of guilt. Are we dishonoring the deceased by being so light-hearted again? Sometimes it's easier to neglect ourselves and our own lives, because we think this makes us faithful to the memory of who we lost. This is much like sailing in circles around the land we found, avoiding the awkwardness of integrating loss and life.

> *We will feel a tension between honoring the world as our loved one made it and changing the world in honor of who we lost.*

We have these pieces of our past, our life before we started to grieve, that linger. A husband leaves a business that is difficult to maintain. Practically, it's time to let it go, to transfer ownership and become free from the painful reminders and the never-ending work. But is he ready? A mother's favorite color was green; when her daughter inherits her home she worries that painting over her mint green wall will erase a memory. This anxiety is normal. We will feel a tension between honoring the world as our loved one made it and changing the world in honor of who we lost.

Ecclesiastes says there is "A time to weep and a time to laugh, a time to mourn and a time to dance."[55] We must grant ourselves permission to integrate healing and remembering. To heal can even mean we are remembering well.

We honor loss by living, and move from remembering one's death to remembering their life. We have noticed that asking ourselves, "What would this loved one have wanted for me?" helps us move into remembering the life of the one we lost. Jonalyn would ask, "What would my mother-in-law want us to feel about her belongings? Guilt? Burden? Or freedom to sell them and take a trip?" Based on Lois Ann's life, Jonalyn and her husband knew they ought to book a trip to the Bahamas.

We honor loss by living . . .

When King David receives word from the prophet Nathan that his child will die, he is overwhelmed, refusing to eat. Scripture tells us that after some time, his servants grow seriously concerned for their king.

On the seventh day the child died. David's attendants were afraid to tell him that the child was

[55] Ecclesiastes 3:4

dead, for they thought, "While the child was still living, he wouldn't listen to us when we spoke to him. How can we now tell him the child is dead? He may do something desperate."[56]

Perhaps David's servants felt like a surgeon who must tell a father waiting in the emergency room that his son is dead. David finally asks, "Is the child dead?"[57] The servant confirms this, likely worried about David's next plunge into mourning.

But David surprises them. Rising, he washes and dresses himself for the first time in days, restoring his normal appearance. When the servants bring him a meal, this time he doesn't refuse to eat. David's abrupt recovery only further worries his servants.[58]

Confused, they ask, "Why are you acting this way? While the child was alive, you fasted and wept, but now that the child is dead, you get up and eat!"[59]

He must go on living.

David, now a grieving father, gives them his explanation. He must go on living. "But now that he is dead, why should I go on fasting? Can I bring him back again? I will go to him, but he will not return to me."[60]

David is not in denial, but likely just as consumed with denial, anger, remorse, and self-loathing as any

[56] 2 Samuel 12:18
[57] 2 Samuel 12:19
[58] 2 Samuel 12:19-20
[59] 2 Samuel 12:21
[60] 2 Samuel 12:23

father would be. Perhaps he was even angry at the Lord's decision to allow his pain. Had he forgotten the tears of seven days and nights entreating the Lord to spare his son? From this time forward, he will likely spend many more nights in tears for his son.

Yet David's words place his loss before God. God has not forgotten. Remembering doesn't rest on our shoulders alone. If the heavenly host knows our loss, perhaps we can feel the weight of remembering shift. God carries our burdens with us. We can ease ourselves out of intense mourning knowing it is not solely our job to honor this loss. God honors our loss forever, saving our tears in a bottle, writing our grief in his book.[61]

> *God has not forgotten. Remembering doesn't rest on our shoulders alone.*

David's words, "Can I bring him back again?" show an honest attempt to make sense of his loss. These words illustrate neither surrender nor retreat. Even as David rides his waves of sorrow, he turns his face to live again, to wash, to eat, to communicate with those around him. Accepting the invitation to comb through grief and be made new. Like David, we keep on living and telling our story because living on the other side is also a way to honor the dead. We can grieve well by living well.

David allowed his grief to pause and right-align him with God and his own vulnerability. Of course, not all or even most of our grief comes as a result of our sin, as David's did, but we can still gracefully allow grief to

[61] See NASB Psalm 56:8

pause our rapid-paced lives. Grief will shake us and leave us confused. But not confused forever. Just like David, we can see the God who rescues us, and receive something as simple as bread, wine, and a clean body.

We can grieve well by living well.

Choosing life after facing death can feel impossible, much like a baby in the womb cannot imagine facing the light and cold of birth. Perhaps we would rather stay in the warmth of the grief we have come to know. A baby in the darkness of the womb is at once in isolation and yet still drawing life-giving care from its mother. The dark and isolating path of our grief is still full of nourishment, from friends, family, and God. And yet, birth must come. And no matter how amazing, birth is always startling. By returning to work, leaving the burial site, laughing again, we are reborn. We become the person who has woven loss into their life.

Grief-work gives us our own re-birth experience. What does life look like now? We wake up on the other side without instructions. When we mourn the loss of a person, we mourn the loss of every aspect of our life they brought out in us. We mourn a future that no longer looks like we hoped.

When Lois Ann died, Jonalyn and her husband had been married almost two years. They grieved the grandmother their children (not yet born) would never know. They mourned the scuba diving trips they'd never take with her, the embarrassing moments she'd never subject them to again. And yet her death completely changed the trajectory of their lives. They studied their legacy in their twenties as most young people cannot afford. They quit their jobs to begin the nonprofit Soulation, dedicated to helping people become more fully human, like Jesus. Because of Lois Ann's legacy, they could cross the globe, speaking and offering themselves to the world. They founded Soulation Press, which published this book on grief, among others.

Jonalyn and her husband died to their old life with Lois Ann, but they live to a new story where her legacy guides them to dare greatly. They continue to talk about how Lois Ann would have loved a sermon they gave, a book they finished, a home they built together. They know she would have delighted in the grandson who knows her as Grandma Lois. Her picture sits in their son's room. They talk to him about her life, just as they talk to him about his living grandparents. And one day, they will take their son scuba diving in her memory.

As we die to our old life, a new one is being formed in its place. We can allow our loved one to alter our lives; we can carry their influence into the future.

We lower our sails and raise the rudder. As we wade to the beach, we are different people, but our change is proof that our loss was real. So real, we walk on shore with a different purpose.

Compass Checkpoint – 6

Read
Home Burial by Robert Frost

1) As you reassemble your story of the one you lost, what are some memories that you feel you bear alone? What are things only you will remember for years to come?

2) What are some memories that you can visit without searing pain? Is anything still searing?

3) How does the idea of carrying your loved one's legacy fit into your grief story? How does it bring your comfort? Does it ever feel like a burden?

4) When have you seen God's power walking beside your weakness? Describe the day and where you were, who you were with, what you experienced.

5) If grief is a death of sorts in your own soul and God is working new life in you, how do you see God re-making you? What is new in your life without your loved one? How do you see your new life blooming in the future?

Watch the film
Rabbit Hole

1) In the beginning of the film, Becca finds it easier to make excuses and avoid a neighbor's dinner party, than to open her grieving to others. How have you entered back into community after your loss? What is the scariest thing about letting others into your pain?

2) In an effort to perhaps spare her feelings over the death of her son, Becca discovers her sister has avoided telling her she's pregnant. Then she discovers her friend has "vanished," feeling a little "freaked out" and not sure how to show support. Eventually, Becca must take the first move to reconnect. Have you encountered a difference in the way friends or family respond to accommodate your loss or maintain their own discomfort? How has this made you feel?

3) During a grieving parent's support group, Becca rolls her eyes as another mother continues to say of her loss, "God just needed another angel." She interrupts and asks, "Why didn't he just make another angel then? He's God, after all." Have you ever felt this way? Reflect on the cliché and well-meaning responses others have had to your loss.

4) Howie accuses Becca of trying to "erase" all the "evidence" of their son from their lives. She's talked about moving, given his clothes away, and insists the car seat be removed from their car. Sometimes decisions for change must be made in order to move forward, but they don't have to mean forgetting or dishonoring your loss. Can there be a middle road between erasing memories and living only inside them? How have you accused yourself of forgetting your loss when you take steps to integrate your own reality?

5) Becca's mom attempts to connect her loss with her daughter's in order to build comfort and community, but Becca feels alienated by the comparison of her four-year-old son's death with the death of her 30-year-old brother to addiction. What is so damaging about comparing losses? What is valuable about learning from each other's loss?

6) At the end of the movie, Becca asks Howie, "And then what?" He lovingly replies, "I don't know. Something." As we move forward in our lives, so much of what's coming feels like an unknown something. What do you do with the tension of "Now what?" Where can you trust Jesus to remake your plans?

Books on Grieving
Appendix A

Books (listed alphabetically by author)

The Last Thing We Talk About: Help and Hope for Those Who Grieve by Joseph Bayly

A Journey of Hope by Susan Beeney, RN (available with other incredible resources at http://www.newhopegrief. org/grief-education-resources/)

A New Theology: Turning to Poetry in a Time of Grief by Sheila Bender

Mourning & Mitzvah: A Guided Journal for Walking the Mourner's Path Through Grief to Healing by Anne Brener *Dying Well* by Ira Byock, MD

Man's Search for Meaning by Viktor Frankl

Final Gifts: Understanding the Special Awareness, Needs, and Communications of the Dying by Maggie Callanan and Patricia Kelley

Grieving Beyond Gender: Understanding the Ways Men and Women Mourn by Kenneth Doka & Terry Martin

Stories from the Edge: A Theology of Grief by Greg Garrett

Hannah's Gift: Lessons from a Life Fully Lived by Maria Housden

A Grief Observed by C.S. Lewis

On Grief and Grieving by Elisabeth Kubler-Ross

About Grief: Insights, Setbacks, Grace Notes, Taboos by Rob Marasco

Before I Say Goodbye: Recollections and Observations from One Woman's Final Year by Ruth Picardie

Grieving: How to Go On Living When Someone You Love Dies by Therese Rando

Surviving Grief . . . and Learning to Live Again by Dr. Catherine Sanders

Never Too Young to Know: Death in Children's Lives by Lois Silverman

A Grace Disguised: How the Soul Grows Through Loss by Gerald Sittser

Grieving the Death of a Mother by Harold Ivan Smith

Grieving the Death of a Father by Harold Ivan Smith

Lament for a Son by Nicolas Wolterstorff

Grief Counseling and Grief Therapy: a Handbook for the Mental Health Practitioner by Dr. J. William Worden

The Art of Condolence: What to Write, What to Say, What to Do at a Time of Loss by H.S. & L. Zuin

Poetry, Plays, and Music for Grieving
Appendix B

Poetry

"To Fight Aloud, is Very Brave" by Emily Dickinson

"A Valediction Forbidding Mourning" by John Donne

"Never More Will the Wind" by H.D. from Hymen

"What the Living Do" by Maria Howe

Collected Poems by Philip Larkin

"Particular Scandals" by Julie L. Moore

I*n Memoriam A.H.H.* by Alfred Lord Tennyson (see XXVII)

The Art of Losing: Poems of Grief and Healing by Kevin Young

Plays

Wit by Margaret Edson

Not God by Marc Straus

Music

"Fire and Rain" – James Taylor
(http://www.youtube.com/watch?v=6AclxTPrEBs)

"What Sarah Said" – Death Cab for Cutie
(http://www.youtube.com/watch?v=ctu0uYL5jlo)

"There's Bound to Come Some Trouble" – Rich Mullins
(http://www.youtube.com/watch?v=HIVX1RHpkrE)

"Timshel" – Mumford and Sons
(http://www.youtube.com/watch?v=kl-VCHzS1So)

"July" – Innocence Mission
(https://www.youtube.com/watch?v=Q3GWtGl11M8O)

"I Haven't Seen This Day Before" – Innocence Mission
(http://www.youtube.com/watch?v=Mg5_O3-5o8k)

Movies on Grief
Appendix C

Amour
Away From Her
Children Full of Life (documentary)
Charlotte's Web
Dead Poets Society
Departures
The Descendants
The Diving Bell and the Butterfly
Extremely Loud and Incredibly Close
Finding Neverland
Ikiru
The Land Before Time
The Lion King
Life is Beautiful
The Lord of the Rings
Marley and Me
Of Gods and Men
Ordinary People
Ponette
Rabbit Hole
Reign Over Me
The Safety of Objects
The Savages
Shadowlands
Sleepless in Seattle
Tara Road
Tuesdays with Morrie
The Tree

Up
We Bought a Zoo
Welcome to the Rileys
The Wind that Shakes the Barley
Wit

Online Resources:

theconversationproject.org – Beginning the conversation about death with those you love

compassionbooks.com – Resources for all types of grief and bereavement

compassionatefriends.org – Bereavement support for those that have lost children

nationalshare.org – Bereavement support for pregnancy infant loss

thegrieftoolbox.org – Resources from the Association of Death Educators and Counselors (ADEC)

hellogrief.org – Grief education and online support community groups

dougy.org – A renowned grief and loss center out of Portland, Oregon

Aubrie Hills is a Thanatologist (CT), wife, and friend to the senior adults. *Charlotte's Web* taught her the brevity of life as a little girl, and gave her the right tools to come home to the death and dying community. Her background is diverse and interdisciplinary, with degrees in pastoral care and literature. She advocates for holistic care for the dying and grieving by helping pen the stories of her patients, facilitating grief groups at New Hope Grief Support Community, serving patients and their families at Hospice Care of the West, and researching the needs of our aging society at USC's School of Gerontology. She and her husband live in downtown Long Beach, California with their cat Carl. She loves to discover classic films, frequent thrift stores, and cook delicious meals.

Jonalyn Fincher is a philosopher, wife and mother. She and her husband Dale lead Soulation, a non-profit equipping Christians to be more fully human. She is the author of *Ruby Slippers: How the Soul of a Woman Brings Her Home*, and co-author of *Coffee Shop Conversations: Making the Most of Spiritual Small Talk*, *Opening the Stable Door*, and *Long Live the King*. Jonalyn writes on stewarding sexuality at her blog hosted by Soulation, RubySlippers.org. She has been interviewed on issues of apologetics and sexuality by the BBC, *The Wall Street Journal*, *The Washington Post*, *Christianity Today* and *BuzzFeed*. Jonalyn lives with her husband and son in the aspen woods of Steamboat Springs, Colorado. She loves to snowshoe in the winter and sail in the summer. Follow @jonalynfincher.

Acknowledgements

We are so grateful for the careful eyes and feedback offered by Becca Shaw, Randi and Eric Peterson, and Tanya Gore, who juggled new babies and new degrees between reading our manuscript. Each brought their own fresh and enduring grief experience to enrich our words. Amy Kaneko, Hawaiian slam poetry champion five times and running, donated her work "Allow Me to Demonstrate You" which describes her own recent loss.

We are grateful for the wisdom and experience of Dr. Terry Martin and the Thanatology program at Hood College, who cultivated and mentored Aubrie to care well for grieving people; for Susan Beeney, director of New Hope Grief Support Community, who introduced the idea of "New Normal" for the bereaved, and whose friendship enriches Aubrie's life's work. Mighty thanks for the collective and raw experiences of friends such as Margaret Graham, Kara Norris, and her hospice patients/families, who so willingly brought voice and/or influenced the stories we shared here.

Martha Byrne smoothed out hundreds of writing wrinkles with her timely and attentive copy editor skills. We are indebted to Jeff Gifford who typeset and designed our cover with the precise theme we envisioned as we started this project. A big thank you to Soulation's Team Manager, Sarah Kappen, who prevented crashes and kept us heading in the same direction. Finally, we are deeply indebted to our husbands, for the tireless encouragement and endless re-reads. Thank you to Joshua Hills and Dale Fincher, President of Soulation, who envisioned this book in the first place. Thank you for supporting, editing, cheering, inscribing the Foreword, and launching *Invitation to Tears* into the wider ocean.